THE COMPL
BOOGER
BOOK

The Complete
BOOGER
Book

Featuring

Ima Picker II

Written by: David E. Nordstrom
Illustrated by: Travis Hanson

Published by

CCC Publications
1111 Rancho Conejo Blvd.
Suite 411 & 412
Newbury Park, CA 91320.

Manufactured in the United States Of America

Cover & Interior art by Travis Hanson

Cover/Interior design, layout & production by Oasis Graphics

ISBN: 0-918259-80-0

If your local U.S. bookstore is out of stock, copies of this book may be obtained by mailing check or money order for $5.95 per book (plus $2.50 to cover postage and handling) to: CCC Publications; 1111 Rancho Conejo Blvd.; Suites 411 & 412; Newbury Park, CA 91320.

Pre-publication Edition - 1/95
First Printing - 7/96

Foreword

After rooting through countless hours of research, it has come to our attention that in today's world of Dead Cats, Practical Jokes, and bizarre animal caricature books, one very important object has been overlooked completely. That, of course, being the ever popular nose candy known as the ***"Booger."*** With this flagrant oversight in mind, our Editors set off in search of Nostrilic Knowledge. Surely you can imagine their surprise when they could not find one single book on the subject. Not only were no books to be found on this favorite American pastime, but to add insult to injury, the word *"Booger"* was not even listed in any dictionary or encyclopedia (although we did find an actual *Booger* stuck to one of the pages). How could this be? It was as if these texts were written by some strange race of creatures who had somehow miraculously rid the world of our all too familiar nose toys. It was as if their intent was to wipe clean not only the world's noses but our entire memory of these favorite cherub chewables. How was this possible? It was an outrage. Why, without *Boogers,* what on earth would a lonely motorist have to do on a long and solitary drive? My gosh, what would kindergarten age children have to snack on? What could we possibly find to replace it as our favorite thing to fling onto the windshields of cars that followed too closely? What else could possibly be used in substitution that would give smaller children a comparable edge when playing king of the mountain? What could even begin to replace it as the mementos left behind in the proof of textbook readership? We were sitting around digging for the answer when all of a sudden it hit us. Yes, that is what we would have to do. Hence, we offer you this, The world's first **Complete Booger Book** in all of its *gory.* Enjoy.

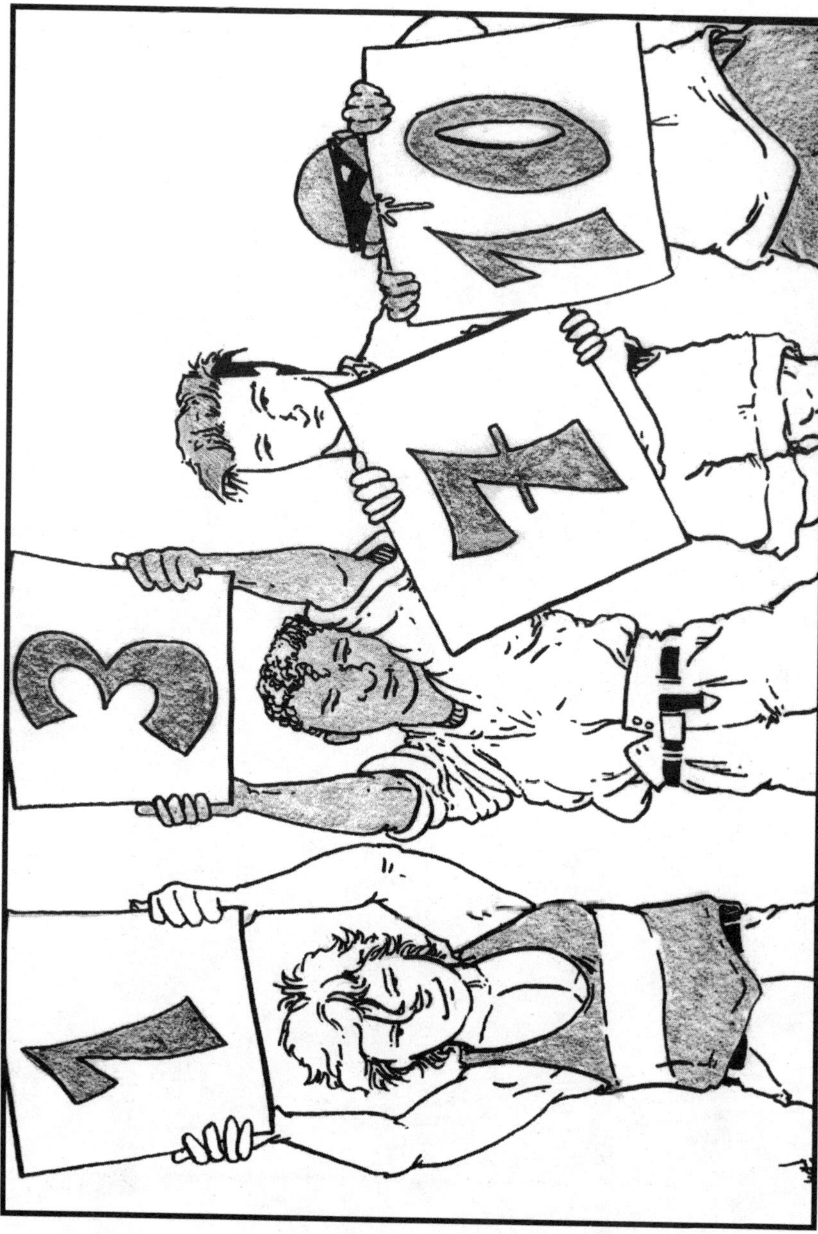
7
3
7
10

THE OFFICIAL BOOGER SCALE

(HOW TO PROFESSIONALLY RATE A BOOGER)

REMARK	SCORE
WAY TOO WET. (ICKY GOOEY) HAS ONLY BEGUN TO BOOG. USUALLY ONLY COMES OUT AT RARE IMPORTANT MOMENTS LIKE A FIRST DATE OR AN IMPORTANT JOB INTERVIEW. OFTEN ASSISTED BY AN UNSUSPECTING SNEEZE.	1
THESE BABIES DEFINITELY CAME OUT OF THE OVEN A LITTLE TOO SOON. AKIN TO A WET STICKY COMET (WHEN ROLLED BETWEEN THE FINGERS LONG ENOUGH, BEGINS TO RESEMBLE A SMALL RUBBER BALL. THE BOTTOM OF THE FOOD CHAIN FOR EVEN THE MOST AVID SNACKER.	3
JUST A LITTLE TOO MOIST TO BE A CHAMPION FLICKER. INTERESTING COLORING. JUST A TAD TOO STICKY FOR COMFORT. A BIG FAVORITE WITH THE PAGE BANDITS. A REAL MEAL WITH ALL THE TRIMMINGS (IT'S SOUP).	5
SEMI-DRY. JUST SHY OF A TRUE NASAL GEM. GOOD SIZE, NICE WEIGHT. CONSIDERED BY MOST PROS TO BE THE CHAMPION FLICKER. ALSO THE TOP CHOICE OF 4 OUT OF 5 NOSE NUGGET DINERS.	7
THIS IS BY FAR THE TOP OF THE LINE BOOGER. HARDEST OF ALL NASAL BLESSINGS. A TRUE NOSE DIAMOND OF THE VINTAGE THAT ONLY TIME AND PATIENCE CAN PRODUCE. SHARP EDGES THAT CAN CUT LIKE GLASS. USE EXTREME CAUTION WHEN EXCAVATING.	10

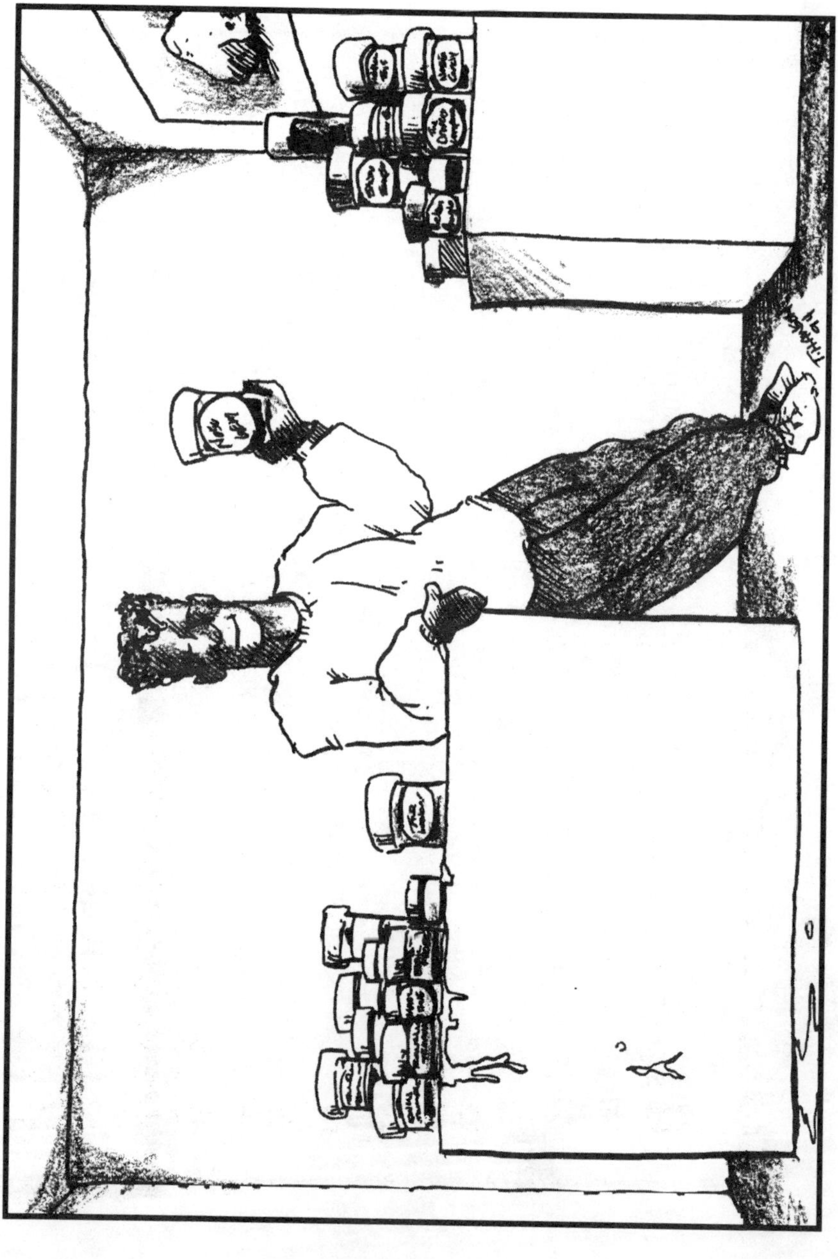

A.K.A. BOOGER

Although we are all familiar with its common title of "Booger," don't be surprised to find it trying to pass itself off as one of these other, less well-known, monikers. The Goober, Nose Gem, Nose Candy, Toddler Toys, Nostril Nugget, Cherub Chewable, Sniffer Snacks, Kleenex Bullets, Button Putty, Pickers Payload, The Driver's Companion, Finger Goo, Schnozz Stone, Beak Pebble, Breather's Bounty, Digger's Dirt, Nerd Bait, Pinky Trinkets, Sinus Samples, Kindergartner Keepsakes, Handkerchief Glue, Traveler's Trophy, The Face Grazer's Delight and, our all time favorite, "The Alabama After Dinner Mint."

THE BASIC PICK AND FLICK

This is your basic pick for the Nose Miner on the run. First a quick rooting, then the inevitable glance down to admire the rushed handiwork. This is then followed by a sharp launching normally utilizing the middle finger and thumb. Great for a picker who's short on time. Of course, you should keep in mind that this lackluster method, although time efficient, greatly reduces the overall picking experience.

6-2=5
MATH IS YOUR FRIEND.
MATH IS GREAT!!
I ♥ MATH

THE HANGER

Also known as the “psyche-you-out-and-make-you-stare” booger. This thing is huge! How can he not feel it? Hell, how does he get through doors with that thing hanging there?! The World record for the longest hanger is held by a ninth grade math teacher in Phoenix, AZ. The hideous thing actually just dangled there for an entire semester and is now credited as the main contributing factor for the record number of high school dropouts in that year.

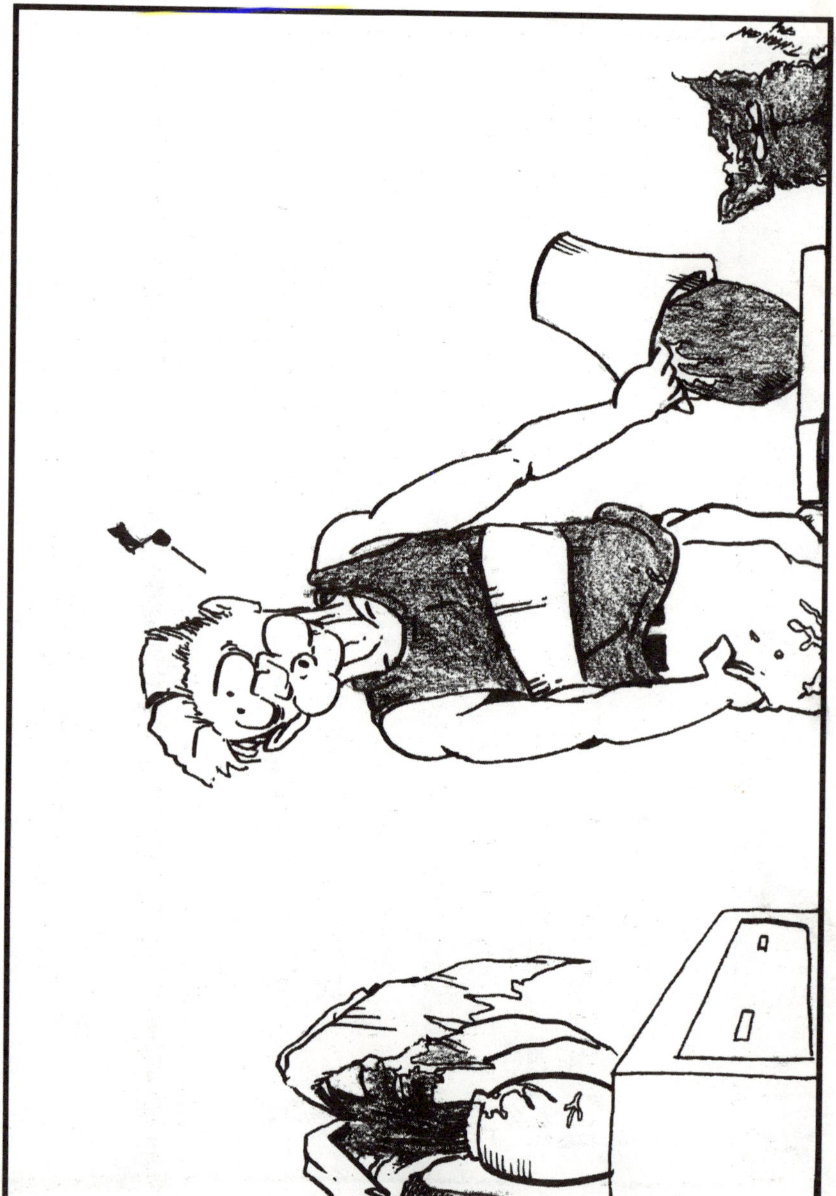

THE PANT LEG SWIPE

Ah, yes, also known as the "tricky picker." The biggest problem with this particular type of nostril harvester is first, you will not be able to forget he has at least one booger on himself if not bushels. And second, the tricky picker will tend to wipe his nose bounty anywhere he thinks it won't be seen (his leg, your arm chair, his own shirttail, your dog's ear.) Your best bet when dealing with this type of picker is to keep your eyes on those hands. Just remember if he's not a pickin' then he's a wipin'.

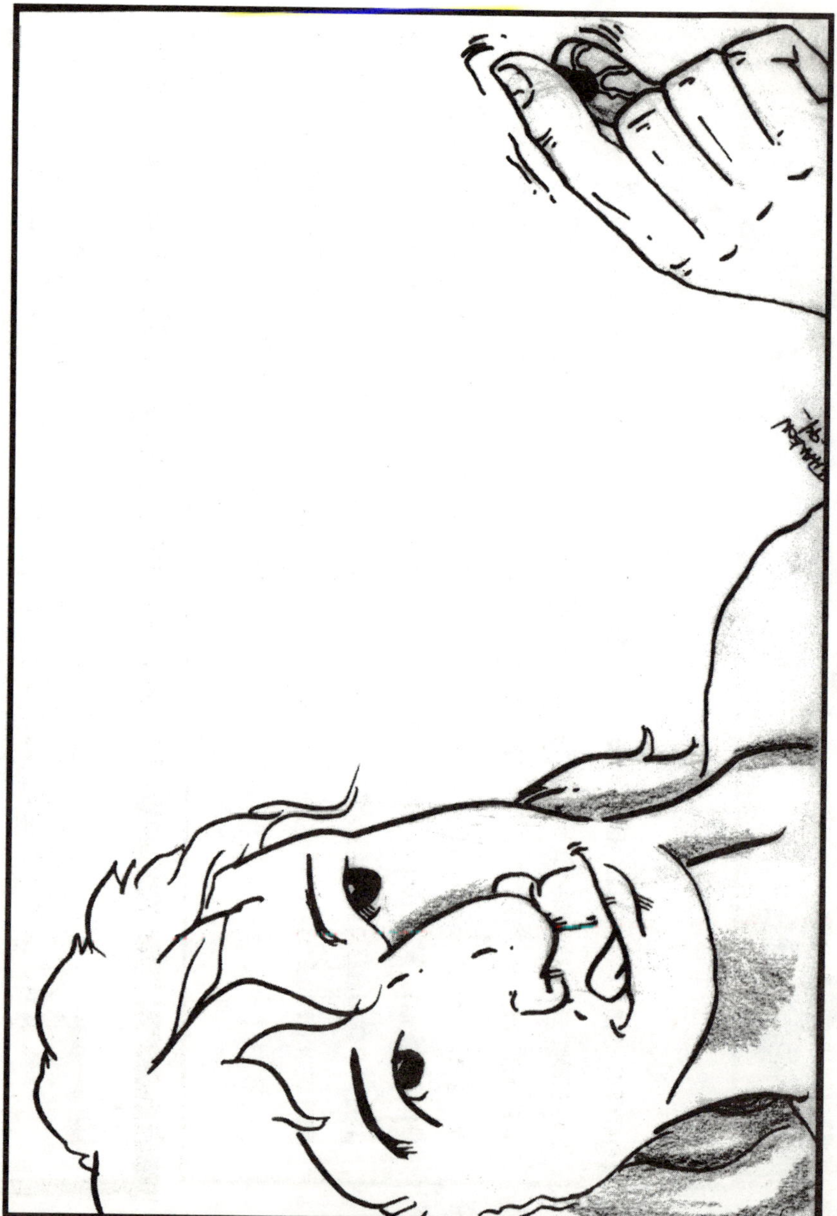

THE ROLY-POLY

Oh yes, Mother Nature's little ball bearings. This particular nose morsel, for some unknown reason, possesses the uniquely lubricated feeling that makes us tend to hold on to it just a little longer than we normally would just to feel it slipping softly through our fingertips. Hey, just remember this, what the hell are you doing playing with boogers? Drop it and get a life.

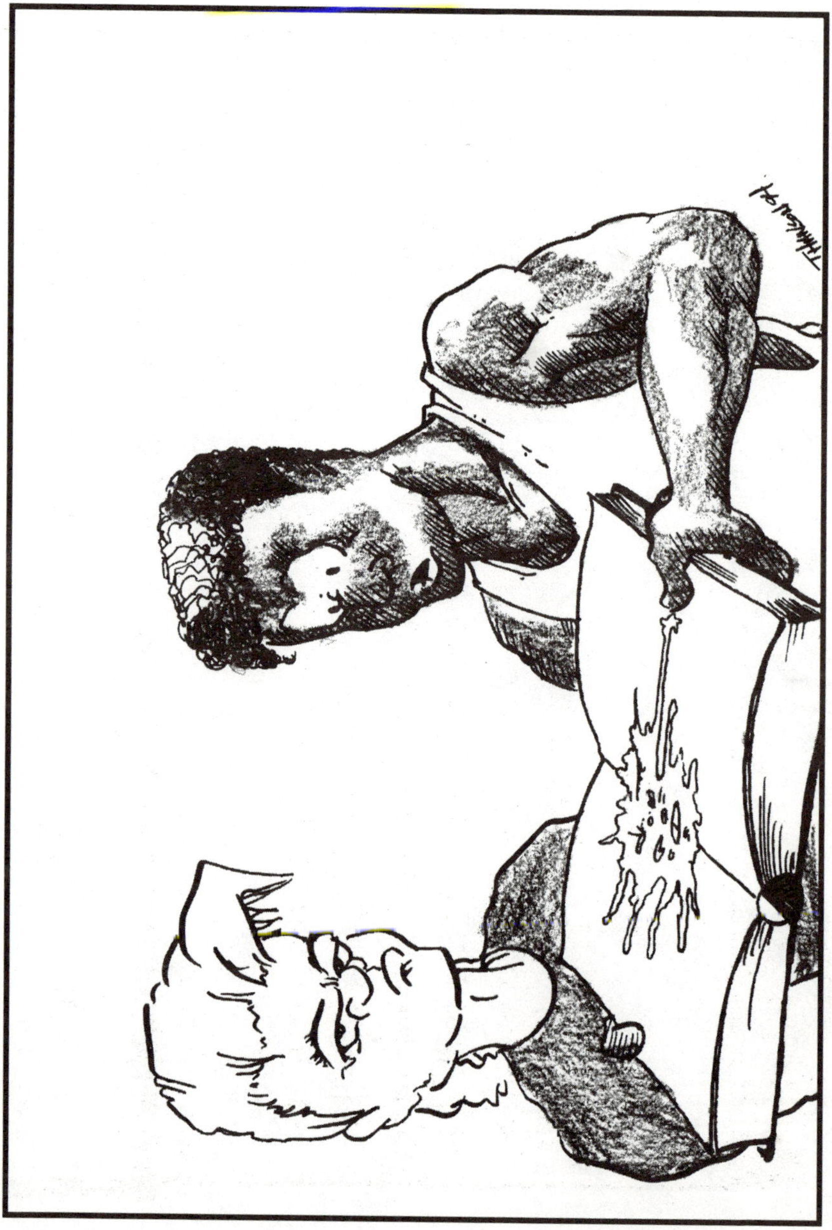

THE BOOK BOOGER

Well, we've done it haven't we? You're ripping along through a good book, you turn the page and there it is. Not only a booger, but the very worst kind – someone else's! It's almost enough to send the book hurling. You ask yourself who would do such a thing? What's the point? Now if you're not thinking that, you're busted, you booger wiper. Shame on you. Get up right now and turn yourself in to the librarian. Now don't you feel better?

THE "HEY, WHAT YA EATING" BOOGER?

By far the easiest and cheapest way of getting a bite to eat. All you have to do is simply pick your nose and walk up to a friend who has some french fries, making sure he sees your quest for the super booger. All you do then is reach in his fries bag, at the same time saying "mind if I have a french fry? Dang, I should probably have washed my hands first, what was I thinking? Especially after picking my nose." Presto, the fries are yours. (Believe me, don't try it a second time, it's only good once.)

THE DEEP DIG

I'm sure everyone has seen at least one of these rare creatures. Most elementary schools come with one as standard equipment. If not, let me tell you, they are surely a sight to see. I will never in my life understand how any one person could possibly get their whole hand all the way in their nose. (I'm talking to the elbow.) At least it sure seemed like it was. Well, anyway, I'm safe now. And if you're out there, the kid from my third grade class who picked his nose *all* the time, you're probably still a freak. Take your finger (or arm) out of your nose!

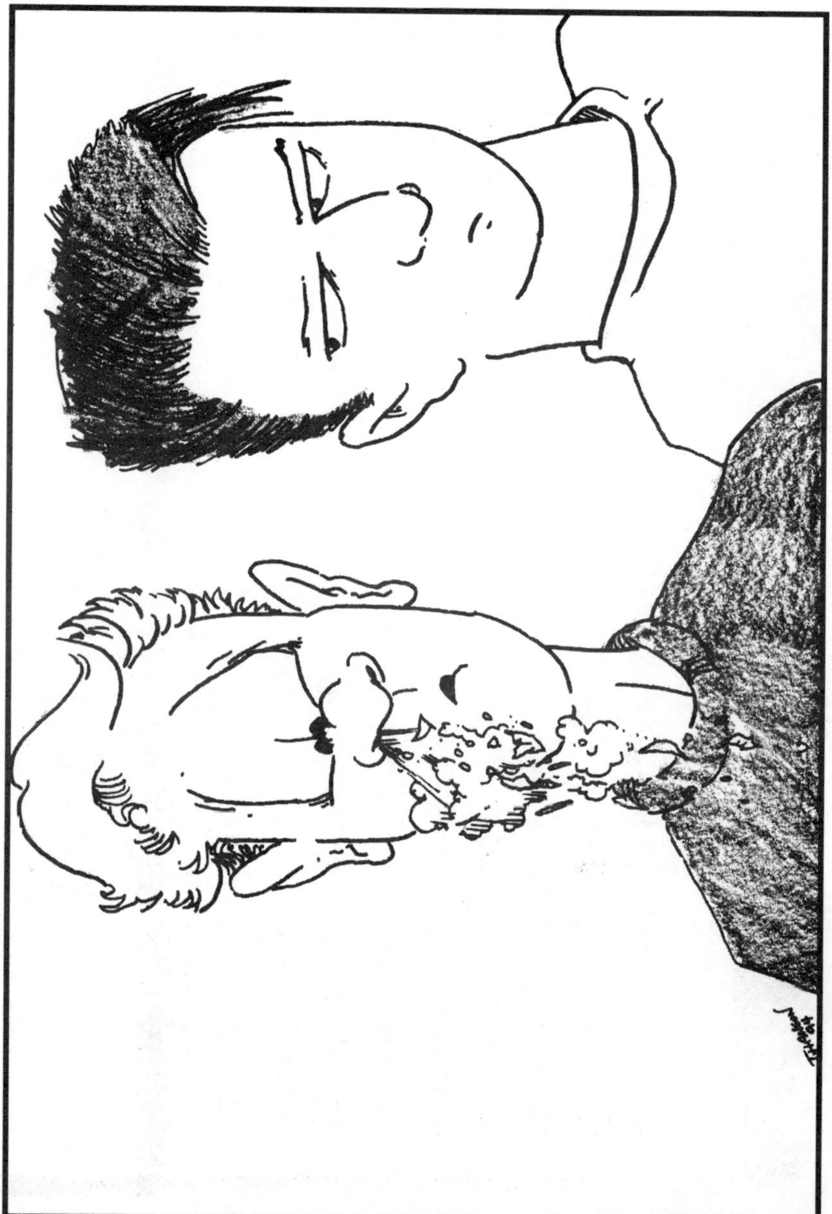

THE CRUSTER

We were not exactly sure if this one qualified as a truly bonified booger, but better safe than sorry. Of course, we are referring to the crusty stuff that becomes dried towards the end of the nostril on a cold day. You know, the stuff that is as flaky as an out of work brother-in-law. After conferring with our expert tasters it was decided that, although it makes a nice garland, the real chow lies far beyond. So brush it off and move on.

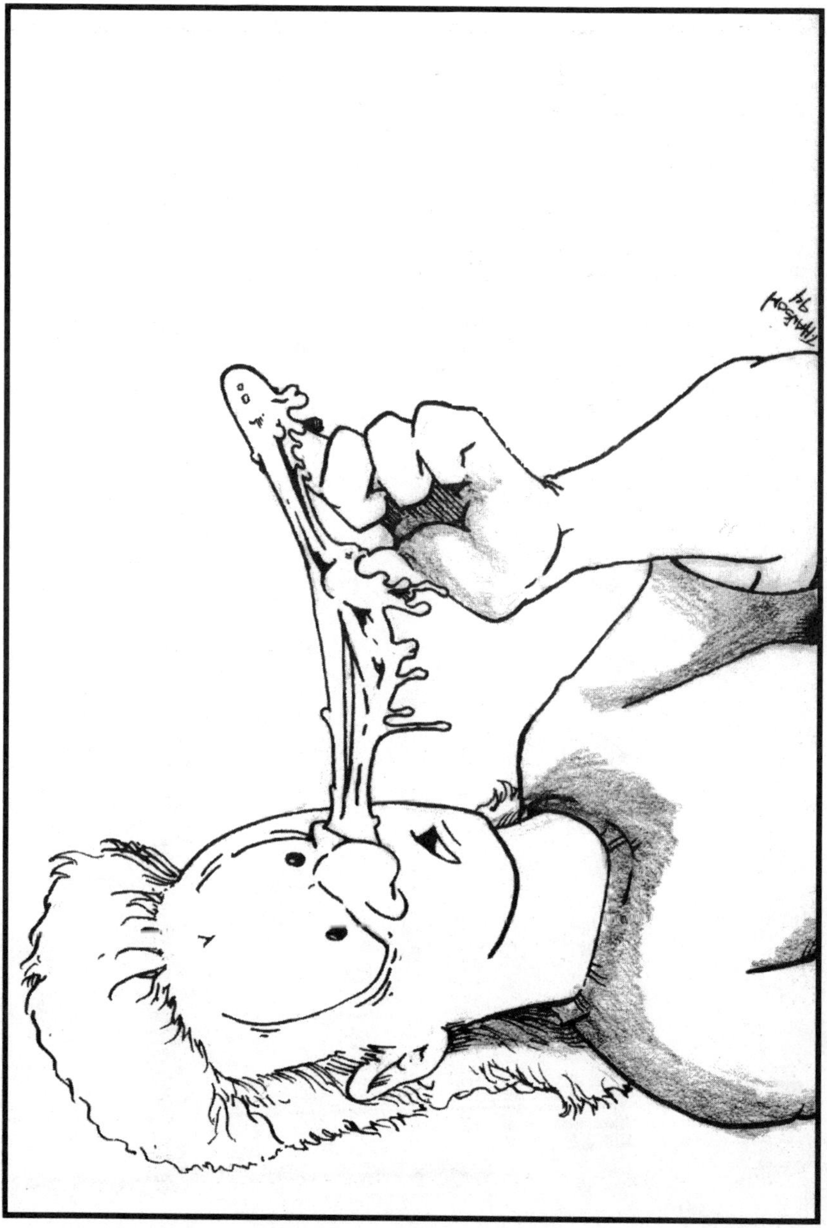

THE SLIMER

Ah, the slimer. Also known as “the booger with baggage.” It all starts out innocently enough. Just a small pick or two, nobody’s watching. Then it happens. Sure it feels like just another small satisfying pick, when all of a sudden it brings with it half the snot in the free world. And, you with no tissue. Now’s the time to see how creative you really are. A little here, a little there, some on the jeans, some on the rug. Next thing you know, you’ve done it again. Yes, you’ve disposed of yet another nose nightmare.

CAJUN STYLE

Well, now we have heard it all. If you have ever swept a garage, or mowed a lawn on a dusty, windy day then you are probably an old hand at our next entry. That's right, it's the blackened booger. Also known as "nostril dirt stew" to those who elect to seek their daily nutritional needs through this less than conventional means. They say a little roughage is good for you. Who knows, maybe one day oatmeal will be replaced by the "Grit Booger."

BETCHA HE EATS IT SCORE BOARD

THE "BETCHA HE EATS IT" ROAD GAME

Now here's a game that's a sure hit with the little ones. To play, all you have to do is find a man who is traveling alone. Now keep an eye out, because if he is not a-pickin' yet, then he's probably just resting his finger for the big Nostril Offensive coming up. Sure enough, after a short wait, the man takes a quick glance around, then heads straight towards picker's paradise. Now, the bet is that he was either simply cleaning out his nose (sure, that's what they all say) or possibly could it be nose snacks??!! Just place your bets and watch.

THE COUGH AND PICK

Now, depending on what part of the country you grew up in, you may or may not be familiar with what is commonly called "the car salesman's slick pick." The way it works is simple. First he coils up one hand into a fist and pretends to cough into it, while all the time he is lifting the customer's wallet. You probably thought we were talking about some new way to pick your nose, but hell, car salesmen do that all day whether we watch or not. And I can't think of anything more boring than a car salesman picking his nose. Can you?

THE FINGER CLINGER

Also known as "the homing booger." Now don't be shy. It's happened to even the best of us. There you are, the model of diplomacy, cool in every way possible. You take a quick check of the nose–don't want anything too weird. Then you detect it, a small booger, top corner, left nostril. No problem you can't handle. You casually reach up and pluck it out with no one being the wiser. Then it happens, you go to flick it away. But no, it likes you. As a matter of fact, it's clinging to your thumbnail as if it had a mind of its own. As you try more desperately to flick it away, it becomes more obvious to those around you just what it is that you are trying to shake. The next thing you know you're known as "the guy with the booger."

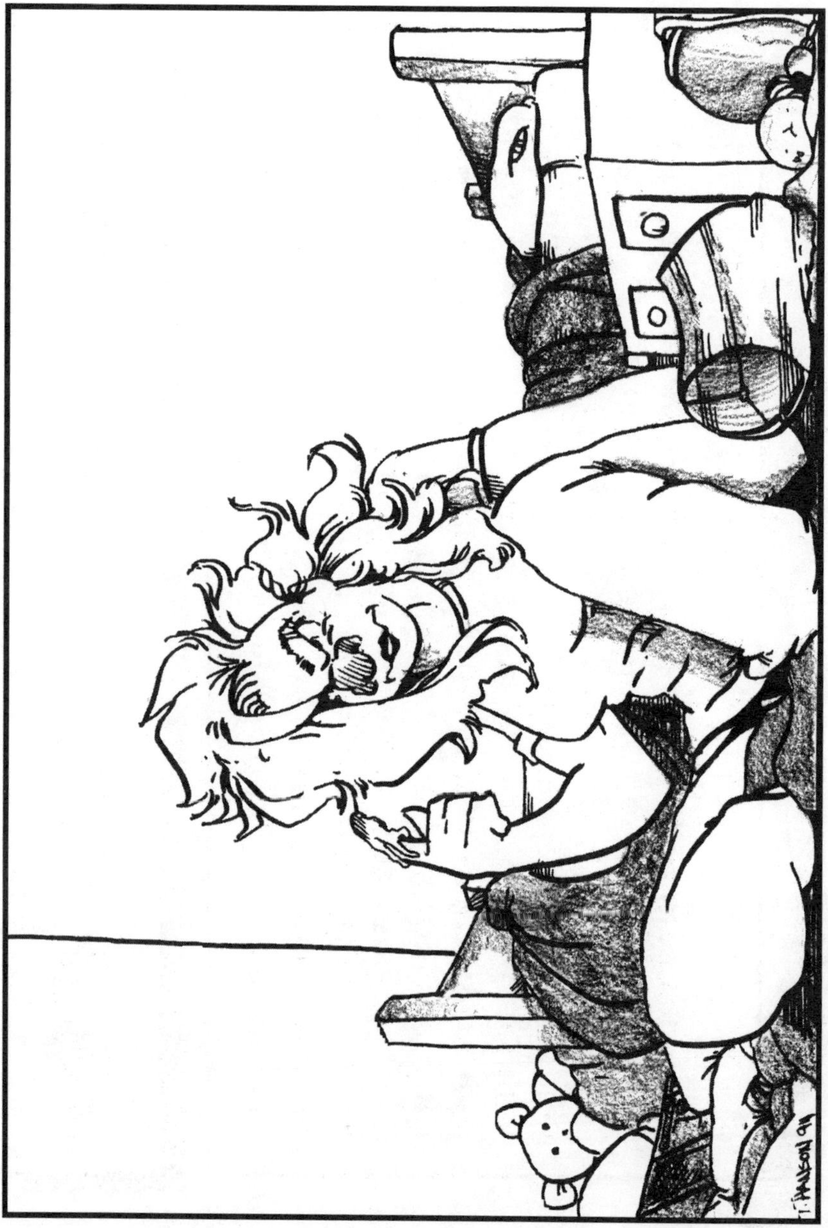

THE STUBBORN BOOGER

It wasn't even a big deal until you found that it was there and wouldn't come out. So there you go, picking at it instead of just leaving well enough alone. After you've been at it for about an hour, your eyes begin watering. And now, since you began screwing with it, your nose has become sore and red as well. As a matter of fact you look like hell, all over one little booger. But, I have faith in you. I know you will get it out of there, even if you have to destroy your health, home and happiness – you'll show that pesky little devil who's boss.

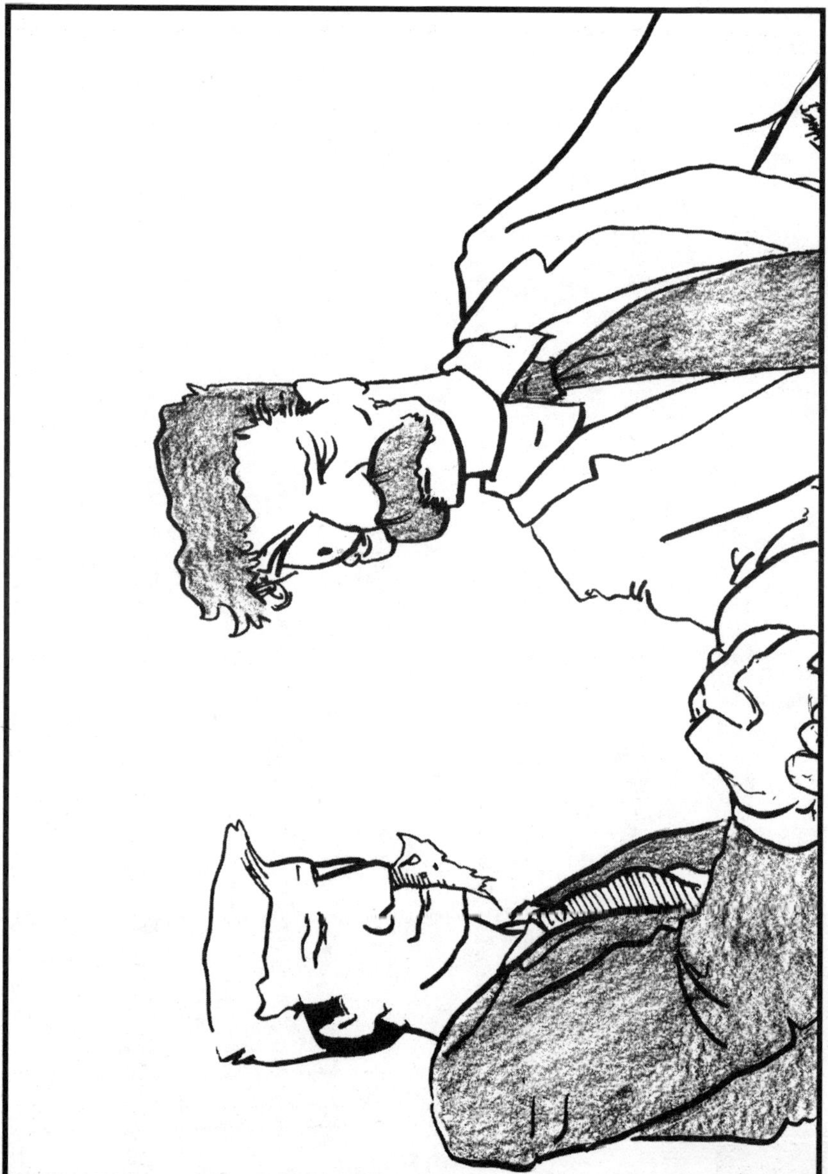

THE PEEK-A-BOO

Finally all those hard years of studying are behind. Yes, you have your M.B.A. from an Ivy League school and in a few moments you will be going in for the biggest interview of your life, the company you have dreamed of working for since you were a young child. You're ushered in. You can feel the blood run through your veins. The interview goes well. You shake hands and prepare to leave. The interviewer is looking at you intensely in the face. He must like what he sees. You're on top of the world, surely you're in. On your way out you stop by the washroom. You take a cursory glace at yourself in the mirror. That's when it catches your eye. With every breath you take, something the size of Texas is popping in and out of your nose. What the hell? No, it can't be! But it is, it's a PEEK-A-BOOGER!!!

THE TRICKY STICKER

It was just a small little booger. You had picked it. You had flicked it and that was that . . . so you had thought. Now it is later, much later. You decide to settle in and watch a little of your favorite TV show. That's when you first start to realize something's not quite right. You're not sure what the problem is, but something just doesn't feel right. You get up and turn on an extra light. Silly girl, it's just a case of the jitters. You settle back in, feeling a little better. Then, as you reach for the remote you spot it there on your wrist. A small, brown, sticky substance. It clings to your finger, it won't go away. Then it dawns on you. You've been cursed with a STICKY BOOGER!!!

THE MOMMY WIPE

This is the first booger trick most of us learn. Normally it happens at about the age of three. Mommy loves us dearly but lately we seem to be embarrassing Mommy. She seems to be hung up on boogers. Not just anybody's boogers, but yours in particular. Especially when her friends come over. She tells you not to eat your boogers. But, if you don't eat them, who will? Maybe that's the problem. Mommy's too old to make her own boogers. That's the answer, you'll just simply share yours with her. — "HERE MOMMY, FOR YOU!"

SALE
SALE ON NEW AND IMPROVED BOOGER REPELLING BODY WEAR

THE SHOOTER

This is the one that has the hardness of a diamond. It comes flying out at supersonic speed when you sneeze. This is one of the most dangerous because it can put an eye out. This little gem can hit a target from 50 feet away. But, because this one is extremely hard, it stings its target rather then attaching to it. These are the ones that archaeologists swear came from the age of the dinosaurs. No new booger could possibly be that hard – so they think. If you have ever been winged by a "shooter," you know just how possible it is.

THE HANDFUL SURPRISE

This is one of LIFE'S exciting little moments that we have all encountered at one time or another. This is where you, having been brought up right, cover your nose and mouth to sneeze. Then, whammy! It happens. You are suddenly confronted with no less than a bucketful of warm "Nostril Goo." In our research we have found that this amazing phenomenon only occurs when the nearest tissue is beyond the fifty-yard mark. Our research also revealed the frustrating correlation between this event and the overwhelming need for someone important to shake your hand.

THUMP
DORKS

THE VOO-DOO BOOGER

As its name well suggests, this *Booger* is loaded with all kinds of supernatural powers. It has been revered through time eternal as one of the most powerful forces known to man. This small yet powerful force has been known to make even the bravest of men tremble with fear. Where can this mystic force be found, you ask? Well you don't have to look far, my friend. They are everywhere. They are simply a *Booger* that comes from the nose of another. (Yuk!)

VOTE
VOTE
T. HANSON© '94

SNEAK AND SNACK

Certainly you have encountered this guy. Perhaps he was your boss, minister, uncle, a respected public speaker, coach, or any one of a dozen people you would least likely suspect. That's when it happens. At first you think it must just be your imagination, but it sure looked a lot like a fingernail chewing that was just way too soon after a nose picking. Then, as you watch, your worst nightmare is realized. Yes, first he does the index finger nose mamba and then, with full cognizance on his part, into the mouth it goes (yuk!) That's right. A full-grown adult, and in public. This is the type of thing that can cause an extreme case of boogaphopia, requiring extensive psychotherapy even years after the actual trauma.

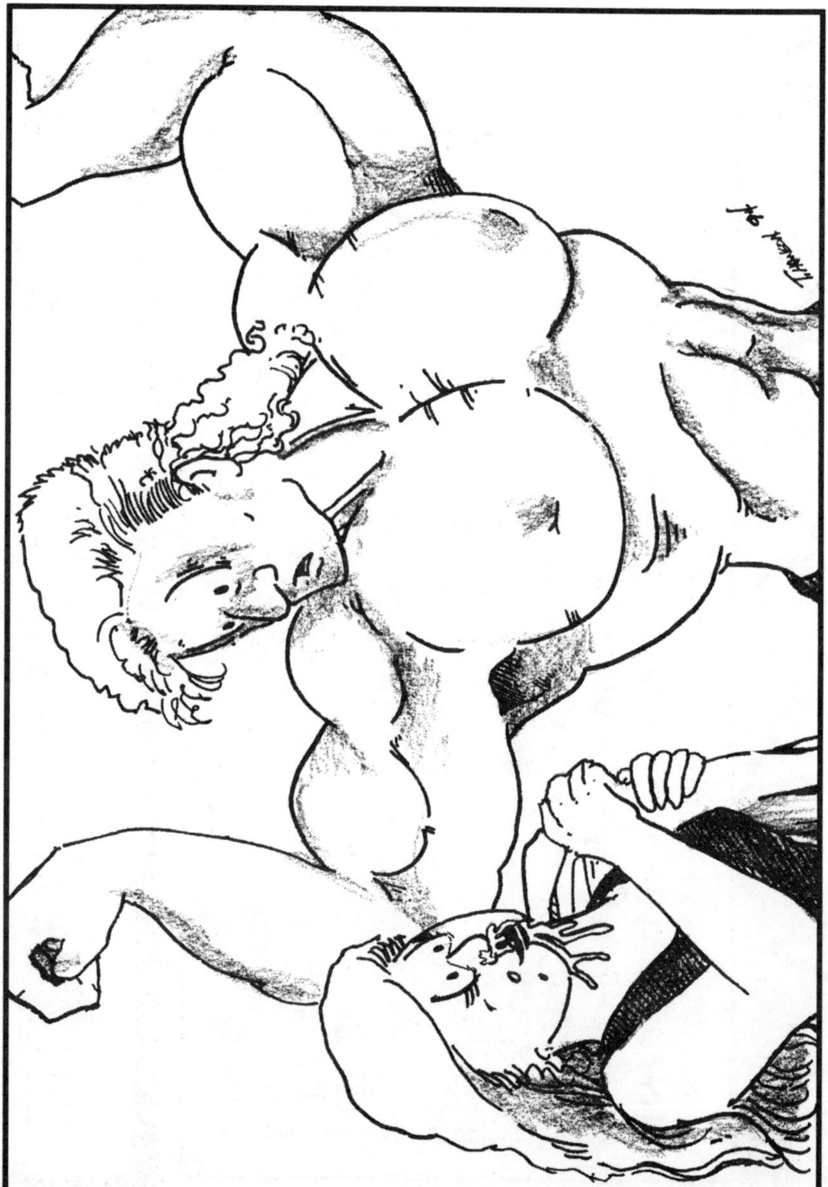

SWIMMER'S COMPANION

Also known as "Surfer's Snot" or "the Boogie Boarder's Booger." We are referring to the less than attractive face additions that adorn the nose of anyone exiting any water activity. This type of nostril event also seems to enjoy showing up at the wrong time. It is almost a sure bet that, directly upon exiting a swim, you will run into that "someone special." And you with what resembles a "Moray eel" hanging on your lip. When utilizing your local public swimming pool, it is best not to dwell on this type of nasal carnage, as it has a tendency to give what once appeared to be a cool, refreshing swimming spot the mental image of booger soup.

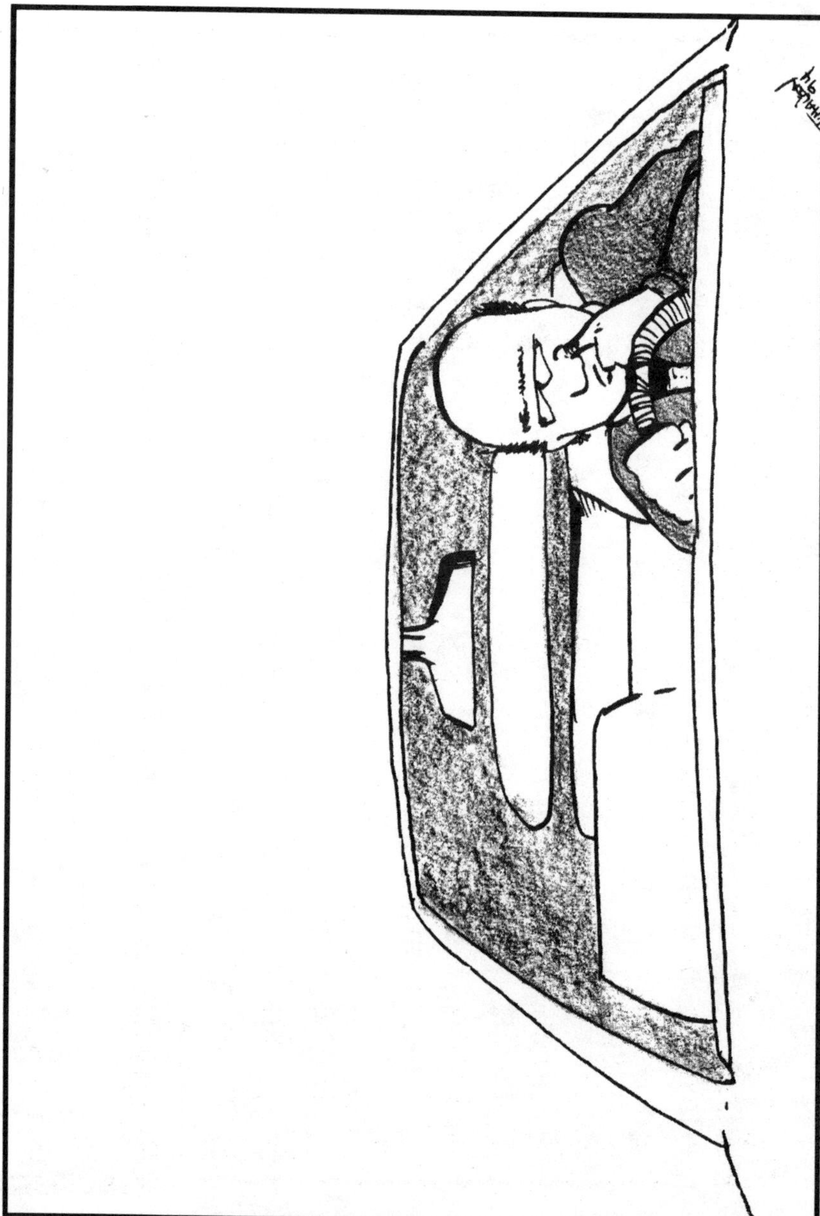

INVISIBILITY BOOGER

This little snot cookie is to be found mostly in men who are between the ages of 30 and dead. Mysteriously, they only work when being excavated from behind a steering wheel. Now mind you, these little nose nasties don't actually make anyone invisible, but they do, however, have the power to make drivers believe they cannot be seen. Hence, these vehicle picksters are convinced that they have become totally cloaked from human view. To witness this remarkable delusion requires only an afternoon freeway drive where you observe the large number of road rooters that seem oblivious to the complete transparency of automotive windows.

THE FACE GRAZER

Both Freddy Kruger and Jason pale when compared to this real-life childhood freakshow. Yes, we are referring to that one kid we all seem to remember from our childhood, regardless of where or when you went to school. This kid really got around and we mean everywhere. This particular "child from hell" was the one who believed that anything that could be picked off the body above the neckline qualified as its own food group. And just as the aforementioned ghoulish zombies are to be found constantly roaming in search of new victims, so too is the face grazer in constant search of new skull snacks. To be considered chow only requires that any normal child is witness to the act. Thus completely destroying any chance of a happy childhood memory of that school year.

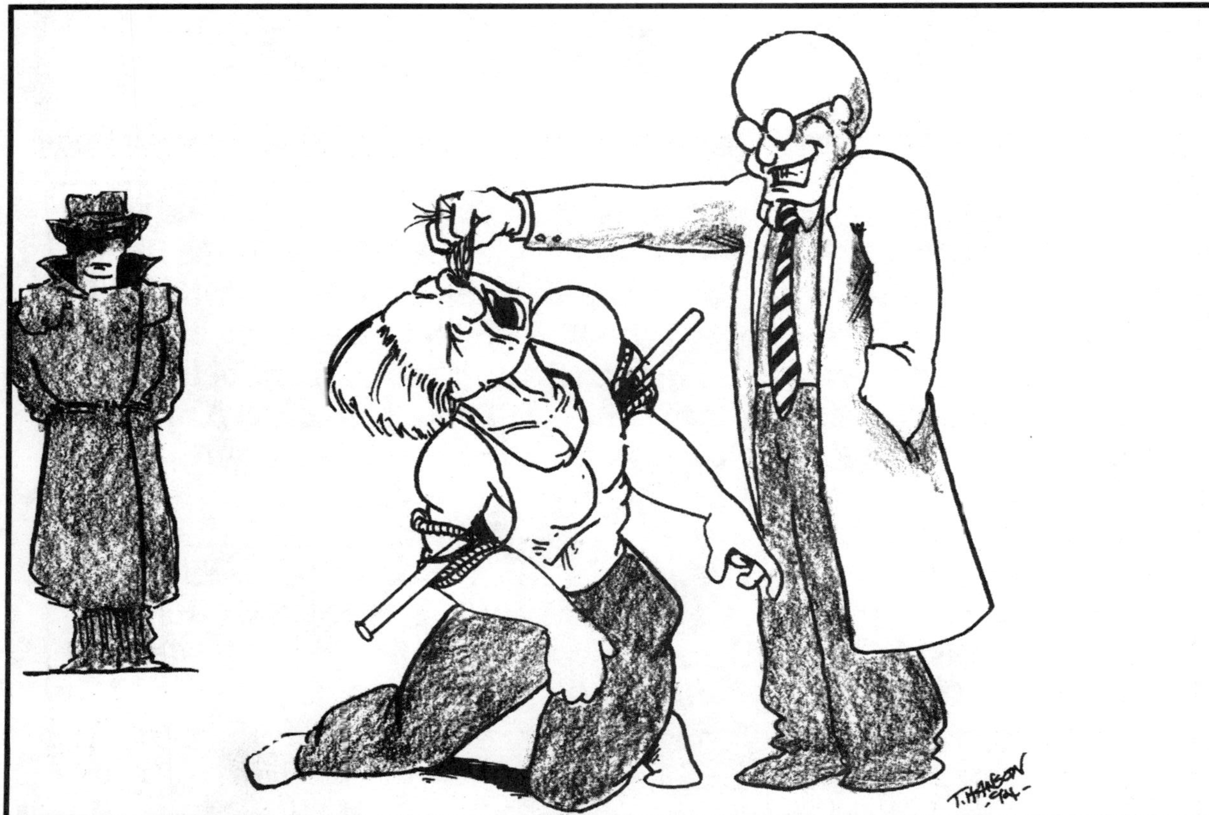

THE PICK-AND-TEAR

This little nasal thespian comes by its name honestly. And you can be assured that just as the shooting of Bambi's mom brought a tear to your eye, so too will this pesky pickster. We are referring to none other than the "Pick and Tear." These little guy's plans are to stay put. As evidenced by attaching themselves with what must be industrial strength epoxy to the small hairs growing within the nostril. Not just any part of the nostril, but to the part which is known to be the most sensitive part of the body by any respectable torturer from the third world. Anyone who has attempted to pick this tear jerker can attest to the brief, yet excruciating pain that could only come from the removal of this type of booger.

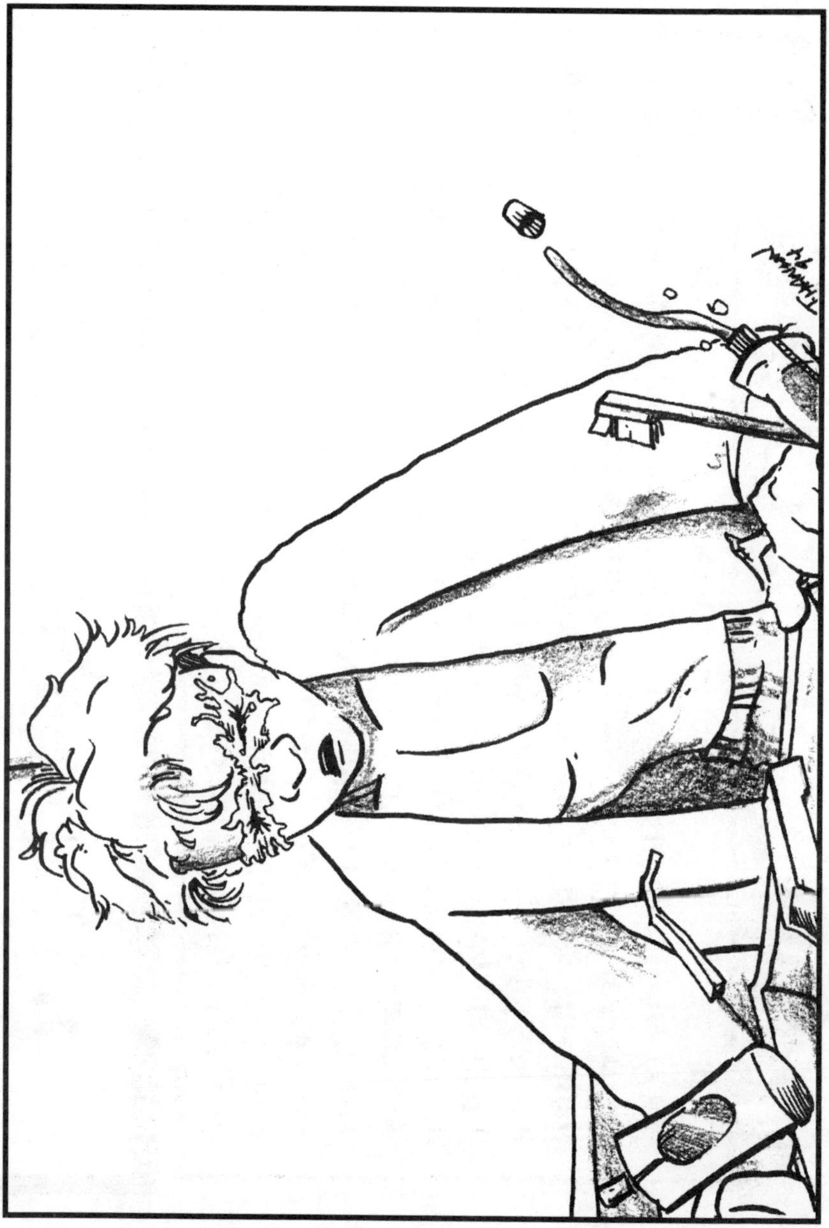

EYE BOOGER

That's right. We are talking about that goo also known as "early morning eye decor." Yes, we are aware that it does not actually rate as a true booger according to the snobbiest of booger enthusiasts. But, because it is a close cousin and will probably never rate a book of its own, we felt it was our moral obligation to mention it here. But, we would like to point out to any children who may be reading this out there that we are booger professionals. DO NOT TRY THIS AT HOME. NOT FOR HUMAN CONSUMPTION. DISPOSE OF PROPERLY. ONLY YOU CAN PREVENT FOREST FIRES. SAY NO TO DRUGS, and always, PRACTICE SAFE SEX.

Thinner Thighs in 10 Days

THE J.F. WORKOUT BOOGER

With this booger, we refuse to reveal the actual celebrity it was named for. We will only point out that she is the daughter of a famous movie star, was not extremely popular during the Vietnam conflict, is married to a man whose name rhymes with "Bed Burner," and starred in a film that started with Barbara and ended with ella. But other than those small clues, you are on your own. This particular nose nugget is actually designed as a dietary aid. Yes, it has only half the calories of a regular booger, and by thinking of the person it was named after, you will probably lose your appetite completely.

!
SNORT!
T. HANSON 94

THE GEEZER SNEEZER

This entry, as anyone who has ever been to Florida near a shuffleboard or bingo area can tell you, is a real life peril that should not be taken lightly. It all begins pleasantly enough. A little easy conversation, you being told how lucky you are to be young and still have your health. Then it happens. First you hear a little sniffle behind you, then an AHHH, AHHH. Finally the inevitable CHOOO. Just as suddenly, you feel something less than kosher hit your elbow. Your head snaps down to see what is what. That's when the nightmare begins. There on your favorite shirt sleeve lies the biggest ugliest booger you have ever seen! You feel faint. Then, from behind you, you hear AHHH, AHHH . . . .

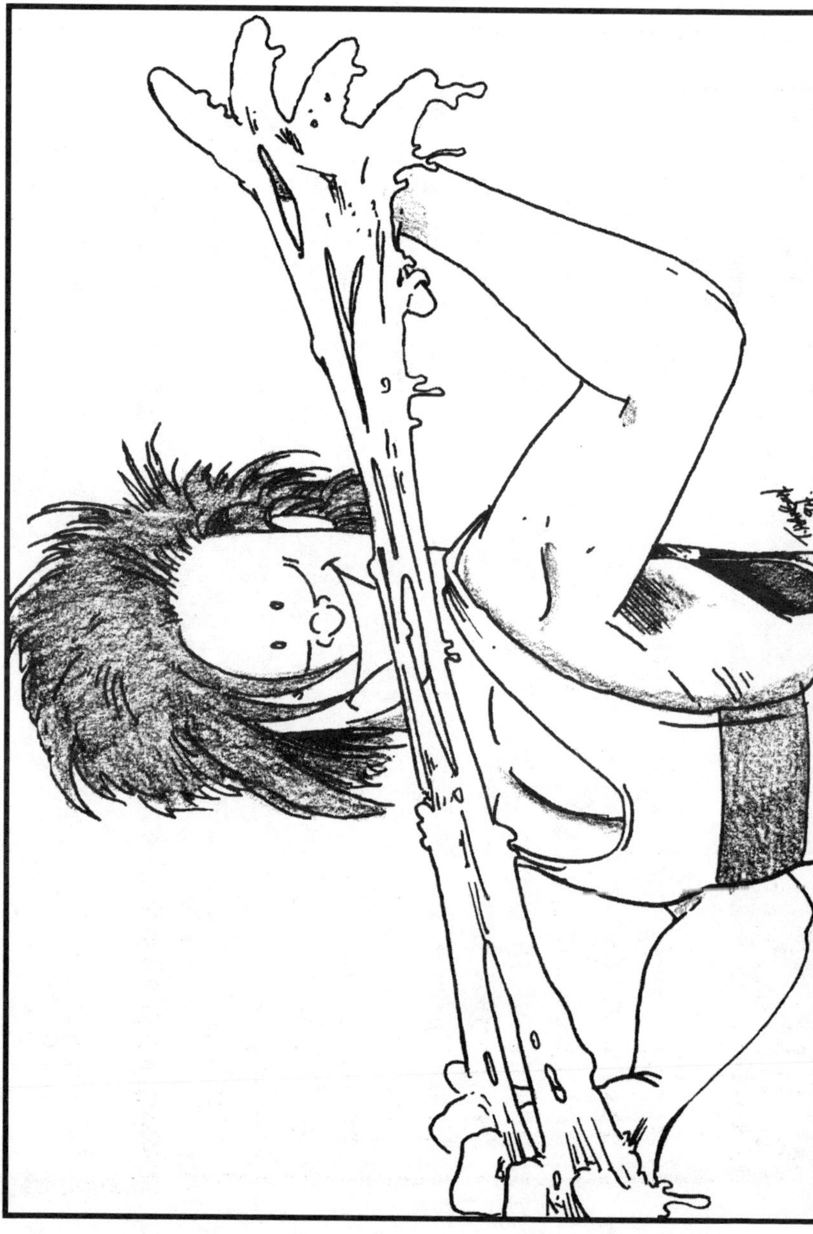

THE BACK AT YA BOOGER

There you are enjoying a quiet moment. Just you, your favorite recliner chair, and a good book. The wife's out shopping. The kids are away at camp. You have the house all to yourself. You had forgotten just how calming a little peace and quiet could be. You turn the page. Suddenly, you are overcome by the desire to beak browse and to your surprise you pick a beaut. Yep, that is a champion booger. After a few seconds of genuine admiration, you have had enough. You warm up for the flick and let her fly. When just as soon as you have flicked it, it snaps back and sticks to your hand. That's when you take that second appreciating glance. Hell, this is no ordinary booger! What elasticity! Why it's . . . it's practically FLUBBER!

THE FART, BELCH, SCRATCH & PICK

Now, what type of booger book would this be without taking at least a few seconds to acknowledge that complete man among men. The Romeo of any trailer park. Yes, we are talking about the very crudest of all the various male personalities known as the beer slurpin', ball scratchin', fart rippin', nose pickin', belch bellowin', feet smellin', unemployed couch potato who makes the rest of us look halfway intelligent. Yes, because of your classless ways and complete lack of charm, you actually make the rest of the male population look like we might have half a brain (although this book is no help in that argument). We salute you!

THE DRIVE AND ROLL

If you are over 16 and have ever driven an automobile, your odds are 99 out of a hundred that you have been a participant in this timeless classic of booger rituals. We are referring to the situation in a vehicle where you have picked or wiped a wet substance from the nose area and are confronted with the now obvious lack of anything to wipe it on. This forces you to begin rolling it around on your fingers until it solidifies. The real experts at this also hang their hand out the window at the same time, thereby disposing of the unwanted substance in record time.

MILITARY BOOGER

There are very few people today who have not heard about the excessive amount of waste and overspending when it comes to the military. Such as their spending $8,000.00 for a hammer, or $30,000.00 for a toilet seat. But few have heard about Harold Winkleman, professional nasal explorer, collector and entrepreneur. Harold, at the height of this military madness, actually convinced a military purchasing officer that an ordinary booger was actually a newly developed gasket material and fetched $450,000.00 for one small sample of his nose findings. Once the government found out what it was, they cracked down on poor Harold by refusing to pay a dime over $36,000.00 per Booger from then on.

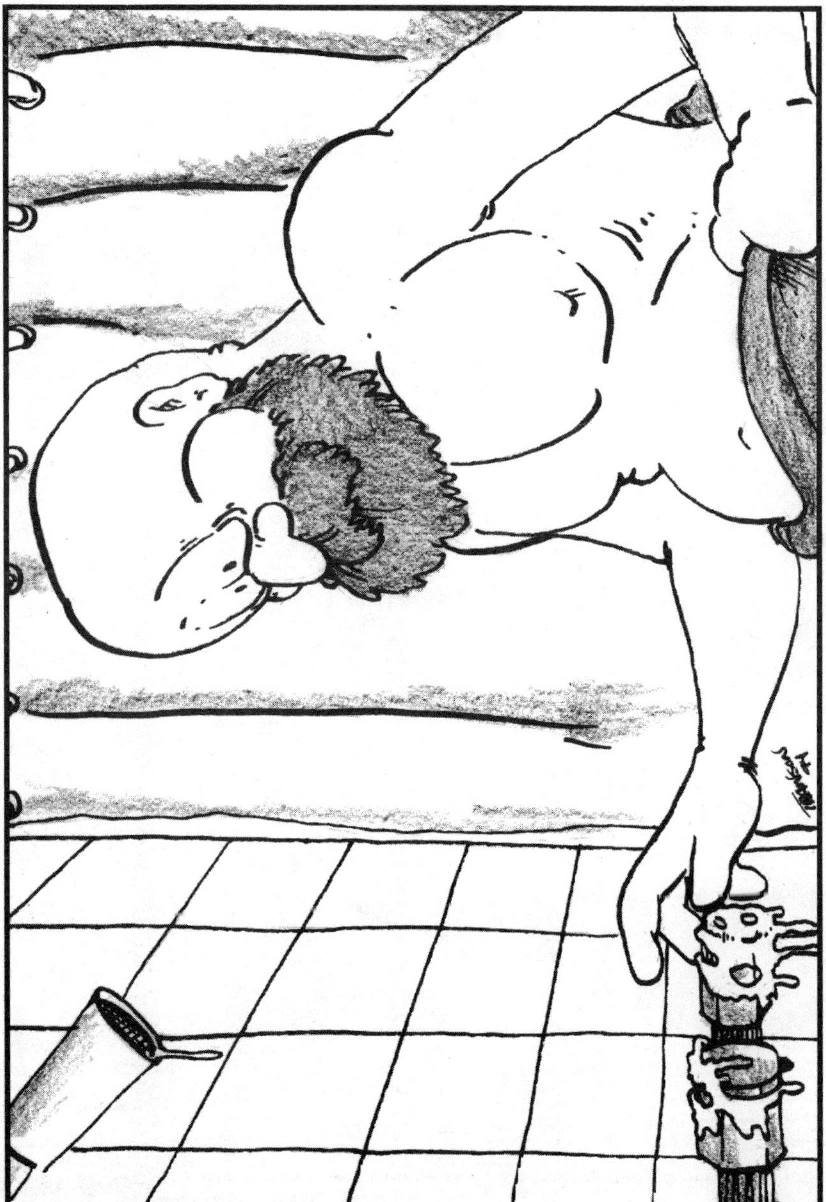

THE SHOWER SECRET

Perhaps secret is not the appropriate term because it is certainly no secret now. When did you first begin this practice of blowing your nose in the shower? What on earth do you blow it on? Certainly you are not going to tell us you blow your nose right into your bare hands, are you? You are the last person in the world we would have expected to pull a stunt like that. But don't worry, we will always be friends with you. We just won't ever want to shake your hand again. You do still use toilet paper, don't you?

THE OVER ACHIEVER

Also known as the "Vat of Snot" or "Sinus Shower," this refers to the phenomenon that occurs whenever your nose has been exposed to extreme cold for any duration longer than a nano-second. At first things seem to be going just fine when, suddenly, you are confronted with the question of whether to start building an ark and loading the animals by two's. We have always found it remarkable that on a cold day a five-year-old child who weighs only 50 pounds can produce twice their weight in snot and not look as though they've lost a pound. But, do yourself a favor and don't touch their sleeve. That happens to be the place that they collect it for ballast.

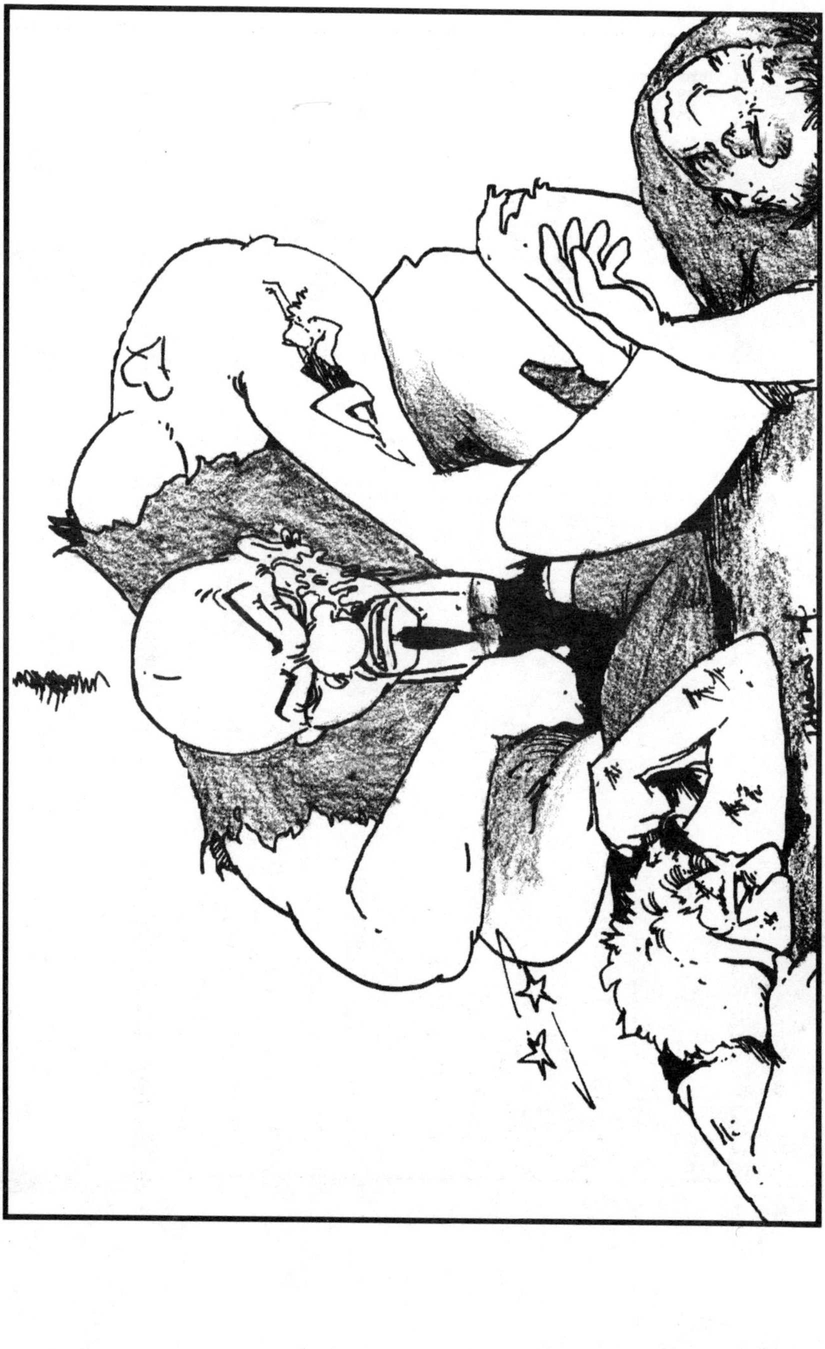

RAGING BOOGER

This is, by far, one of the biggest booger blunders possible and one that will more than likely never be forgotten or forgiven. We are referring to none other than the faulty flick. The way this unfortunate event unfolds is as follows: You are innocently strolling along. Upon a check of the nostril, a large booger is detected, excavated, and what you think will be a routine disposal turns into a nosepicker's nightmare. Suddenly the best laid plans go awry and your flicked folly ends up sticking to the face of a passing body builder who is as big as the lie "I smoked it but I didn't inhale." He then proceeds to beat you senseless. Remember, boogers are not a toy. Lock them and all firearms away from children.

BOOGERJITSU

This was actually the very honored and humble beginning to all of today's Oriental martial arts. Once practiced by only the elite of Samurai warriors, the cool thing about this martial art was there was no flipping, hitting or kicking. It was all done booger to booger in a battle to the touch. This became so unbearable to these ancient warriors, that they eventually decided it was better to get kicked in the face, than touched by a booger. Even today this rare-yet-effective Oriental art is known to only a few select masters, for fear that it is just too much power to let go unchecked in the hands of lesser men. If you remember the TV show Kung Fu, actually it was not a pebble he was trying to snatch from his masters hand, but an ancient Samurai booger. That is why it took so long for a young man with good vision to grab it from an old blind guy.

FAMOUS BOOGER MOMENTS

Most people just take boogers for granted, not really taking the time to realize the many important moments throughout time that boogers were actually involved in one form or another. Why, anywhere man has been, our friend the booger was right there with us every step of the way. If you just stop and think about it, they were even on the moon with the astronauts providing companionship as well as between meal snacks. As a matter of fact, Neil Armstrong said another quotable first up on the moon which has gone, until now, unrecorded: "This is one small pick for man, one giant leap for nose-kind. Now pass the Tang."

BOOGER
RECIPE
SECRET
T. HANSON
94

THE SECRET RECIPE

In order to offer what we believe to be the exact recipe for boogers, we went in search of nerds and kindergarten age children around the globe. Our final conclusions were, that no one was exactly sure of the specific ingredients. But one finding was unanimous, the longer in the nose the firmer these little mysteries become. It was even brought to our attention that you could control, through practiced patience, whether or not they came out original style or extra crispy. We are sure that there are scientists somewhere who hold the magic key to knowledge in this area. But as of now, they're not talking.

WARNIN
DANGER

DANGER BOOGERS

As you have probably noticed, boogers do not come with any type of warning labels. It is kind of a "proceed at your own risk" proposition. This being the case, we have put together a few of the basic facts we discovered while we performed our research. (1) If you eat anything that comes off or around your head, you are a huge nerd and nobody likes you. (2) If you are a man and are driving alone, it is mandatory in some states that you pick your nose or you will be cited. (3) If you are still engaging in these activities, you need first to be introduced to a box of tissue and, second, get professional help. (4) If you make someone real mad while you are picking your nose, you are likely to end up with both a broken nose and a broken finger, so be careful!

WORLDS
1st
40 lbs
Booger

BOOGER STATISTICS

After searching both high and low we came to discover that there just is not anyone out there who keeps accurate records where boogers are concerned. We did, however, hear quite a bit of what we believe could only be propaganda circulated by those individuals who feel boogers are not getting a fair rap. We heard such rumors as one young lad in Arkansas who is said to have lived off nothing more than his nose pickings for two years and somehow managed to gain 64 pounds. There is also the tall tale of the forty-one pound booger that was picked during the World's Fair. But other than these tidbits of unsubstantiated claims, we found no more than a world of people who thought we were really weird just for asking. Go figure.

THE BOOGER BLUES

Booger fanciers tend to have one thing in common and that, aside from spending a lot of time with their fingers up their nose, is music and especially the blues. For some unknown reason they just tend to gravitate in this direction. Your preference on this type of music says an awful lot about your picker's status. Every nose likes music and each and every one of them shows it from time to time by going out and blowing a little boogie. (Sorry, but we had to do it, after all it is a *Booger Book*.)

Pickers Creed

PICKER'S CREED

FRATERNAL ORDER OF THE NOSE AND FINGER

I, being a nose picker of the world, do hereby solemnly swear to dedicate myself in the useless pursuit of nasal clearing on a full-time basis. I swear to give extra attention to my nose cavity whenever I find myself located anywhere near traffic or a car. I further do hereby swear that I will do my best to pick, with extra zeal, whenever I am being observed by anyone, especially those I do not yet know. I swear to be especially geek-like, therefore assuring that my picking time is never infringed upon by the opposite sex. I will treat all boogers as I would want them to treat me. I will consume large quantities of my own boogers and will deny it to all that ask or accuse. I do hereby swear upon this empty box of tissue.

E PLURIBUS BOOGERUS IN DICTI PICITUS UNUM

TITLES BY CCC PUBLICATIONS

Retail $4.99
"?" book
POSITIVELY PREGNANT
WHY MEN ARE CLUELESS
CAN SEX IMPROVE YOUR GOLF?
THE COMPLETE BOOGER BOOK
FLYING FUNNIES
MARITAL BLISS & OXYMORONS
THE VERY VERY SEXY ADULT DOT-TO-DOT BOOK
THE DEFINITIVE FART BOOK
THE COMPLETE WIMP'S GUIDE TO SEX
THE CAT OWNER'S SHAPE UP MANUAL
PMS CRAZED: TOUCH ME AND I'LL KILL YOU!
RETIRED: LET THE GAMES BEGIN
THE OFFICE FROM HELL
FOOD & SEX
FITNESS FANATICS
YOUNGER MEN ARE BETTER THAN RETIN-A
BUT OSSIFER, IT'S NOT MY FAULT

Retail $4.95
YOU KNOW YOU'RE AN OLD FART WHEN...
1001 WAYS TO PROCRASTINATE
HORMONES FROM HELL II
SHARING THE ROAD WITH IDIOTS
THE GREATEST ANSWERING MACHINE MESSAGES OF ALL TIME
WHAT DO WE DO NOW?? (A Guide For New Parents)
HOW TO TALK YOU WAY OUT OF A TRAFFIC TICKET
THE BOTTOM HALF (How To Spot Incompetent Professionals)
LIFE'S MOST EMBARRASSING MOMENTS
HOW TO ENTERTAIN PEOPLE YOU HATE
YOUR GUIDE TO CORPORATE SURVIVAL
THE SUPERIOR PERSON'S GUIDE TO EVERYDAY IRRITATIONS
GIFTING RIGHT

Retail $5.95
LOVE DAT CAT
CRINKLED 'N' WRINKLED
SIGNS YOU'RE A GOLF ADDICT
SMART COMEBACKS FOR STUPID QUESTIONS
YIKES! IT'S ANOTHER BIRTHDAY
SEX IS A GAME
SEX AND YOUR STARS
SIGNS YOUR SEX LIFE IS DEAD
40 AND HOLDING YOUR OWN
50 AND HOLDING YOUR OWN
MALE BASHING: WOMEN'S FAVORITE PASTIME
THINGS YOU CAN DO WITH A USELESS MAN
MORE THINGS YOU CAN DO WITH A USELESS MAN
THE WORLD'S GREATEST PUT-DOWN LINES
LITTLE INSTRUCTION BOOK OF THE RICH & FAMOUS
WELCOME TO YOUR MIDLIFE CRISIS
GETTING EVEN WITH THE ANSWERING MACHINE
ARE YOU A SPORTS NUT?
MEN ARE PIGS / WOMEN ARE BITCHES
ARE WE DYSFUNCTIONAL YET?
TECHNOLOGY BYTES!
50 WAYS TO HUSTLE YOUR FRIENDS ($5.99)
HORMONES FROM HELL
HUSBANDS FROM HELL
KILLER BRAS & Other Hazards Of The 50's
IT'S BETTER TO BE OVER THE HILL THAN UNDER IT
HOW TO REALLY PARTY!!!
WORK SUCKS!
THE PEOPLE WATCHER'S FIELD GUIDE
THE UNOFFICIAL WOMEN'S DIVORCE GUIDE
THE ABSOLUTE LAST CHANCE DIET BOOK
FOR MEN ONLY (How To Survive Marriage)
THE UGLY TRUTH ABOUT MEN
NEVER A DULL CARD
RED HOT MONOGAMY (In Just 60 Seconds A Day) ($6.95)
HOW TO SURVIVE A JEWISH MOTHER ($6.95)
WHY MEN DON'T HAVE A CLUE ($7.99)
LADIES, START YOUR ENGINES! ($7.99)

Retail $3.95
NO HANG-UPS
NO HANG-UPS II
NO HANG-UPS III
HOW TO SUCCEED IN SINGLES BARS
HOW TO GET EVEN WITH YOUR EXES
TOTALLY OUTRAGEOUS BUMPER-SNICKERS ($2.95)

NO HANG-UPS – CASSETTES Retail $4.98
Vol. I: GENERAL MESSAGES (Female)
Vol. I: GENERAL MESSAGES (Male)
Vol. II: BUSINESS MESSAGES (Female)
Vol. II: BUSINESS MESSAGES (Male)
Vol. III: 'R' RATED MESSAGES (Female)
Vol. III: 'R' RATED MESSAGES (Male)
Vol. IV: SOUND EFFECTS ONLY
Vol. V: CELEBRI-TEASE

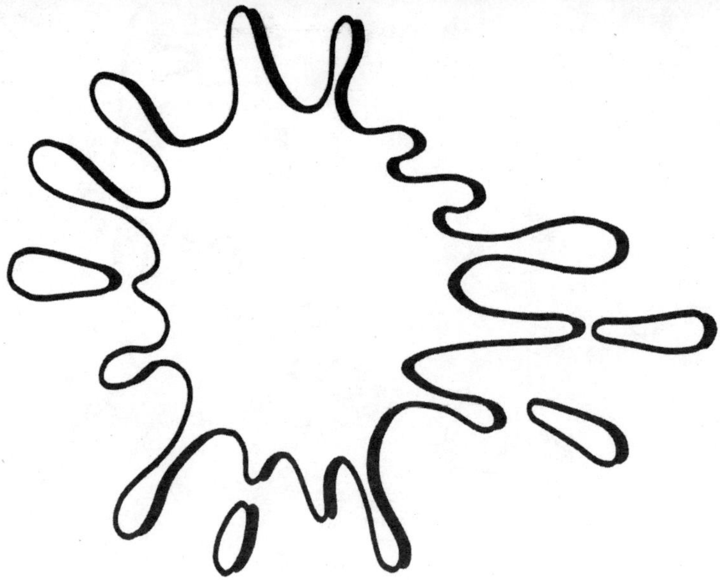